Christian Meditations
Adult Coloring Book

Pictures by Jerry D. Clement
Meditations by Jacquelyn Lynn

Christian Meditations

Adult Coloring Book

Publisher: Tuscawilla Creative Services, LLC
Cover Design: Jerry D. Clement
Production and Composition: Tuscawilla Creative Services

Copyright © 2017 by Jacquelyn Lynn & Jerry D. Clement

All rights reserved. No part of this publication may be reproduced, distributed or transmitted in any form or by any means, without prior written permission.

Tuscawilla Creative Services, LLC
P. O. Box 1501
Goldenrod, FL 32733-1501

www.CreateTeachInspire.com

For bulk purchase information, including customization options, email info@contacttcs.com

Christian Meditations Adult Coloring Book / Jacquelyn Lynn & Jerry D. Clement

ISBN: 978-1-941826-17-1

Shout for joy to God, all the earth!
Psalm 66:1 (NIV)

The initial plan for our adult coloring books was to create drawings from Jerry's photographs of God's world, giving a wider audience the chance to appreciate his artistry while adding their own individual touch to those images.

We shared our plan with a number of friends while it was still in the development stage. Alyssa Kirwan told us that what she would appreciate and had been unable to find was an adult coloring book with Christian messages accompanying each image so that she could meditate on them as she colored.

We loved the idea! And *Christian Meditations* was born.

When we shared that concept with Virginia Bibliowicz, she loved it, too—and immediately took the role of head cheerleader, keeping us on track and coming up with great marketing ideas.

Our original design had one image and a meditation on each page. After we created *Faith Words*, our second adult coloring book, we decided to revise *Christian Meditations* to make the text of the meditations colorable images as well. This allowed us to double the number of colorable pictures and provide an even richer coloring experience for you.

We are thankful for the love and support of Alyssa, Virginia and all of our family and friends. We hope you will be as blessed by the images and messages in this coloring book as we were by creating them for you.

Jerry D. Clement
Jacquelyn Lynn

Acknowledge and take to heart this day that the Lord is God in heaven above and on the earth below. There is no other.

Deuteronomy 4:39 (NIV)

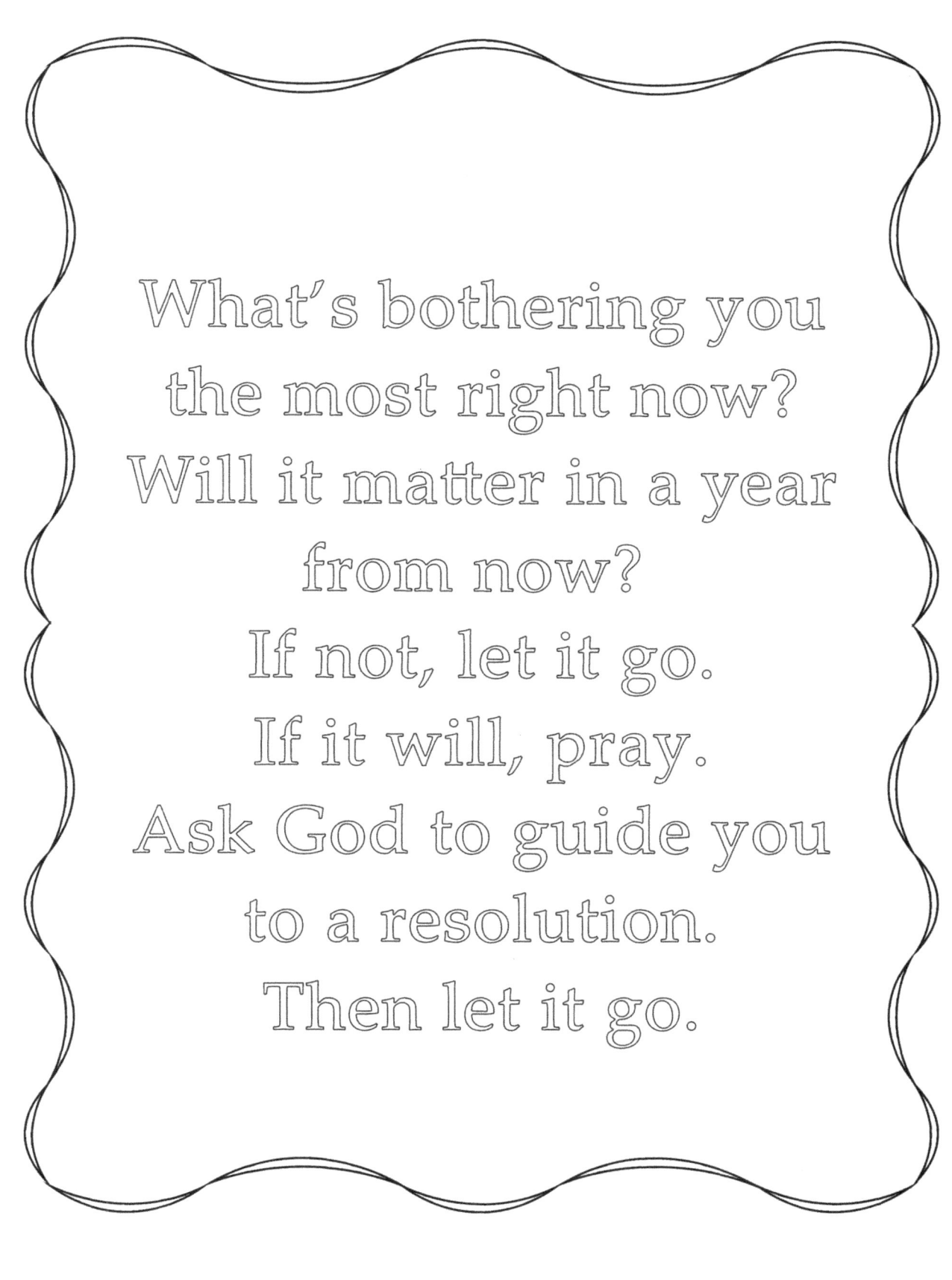

What's bothering you the most right now?
Will it matter in a year from now?
If not, let it go.
If it will, pray.
Ask God to guide you to a resolution.
Then let it go.

No matter how much you know, there will always be more to learn.

Open your eyes and your heart to the abundance of teachers God has placed in your world who are waiting to share what they know.

When you're feeling impatient, chances are it's because you're trying to make things happen on your schedule. Remember that things are going to work on God's time, not yours. Ask God for the patience to wait until His time is right.

Life is not about success
or failure, it's about results.
Don't think about whether
you succeeded or failed,
think about the results
you produced
Were they what you wanted?
Were they what you expected?
What would you change?
Most important, were
the results part
of God's plan for you?

Every time you're feeling like things are so tough that you want to give up because you can't make it through, remember that you've made it through until now. You've got a great track record of surviving the tough times. Ask God for the strength you need and keep going. You'll survive again.

Are you frustrated and stressed because you didn't get everything done today? You got everything done that you were supposed to get done. Advice for tomorrow: Relax and let God be in control. You may not complete your plan, but you will live out His.

If you died today, what would you regret? What would you feel you left undone? It's not too late to do something about it.

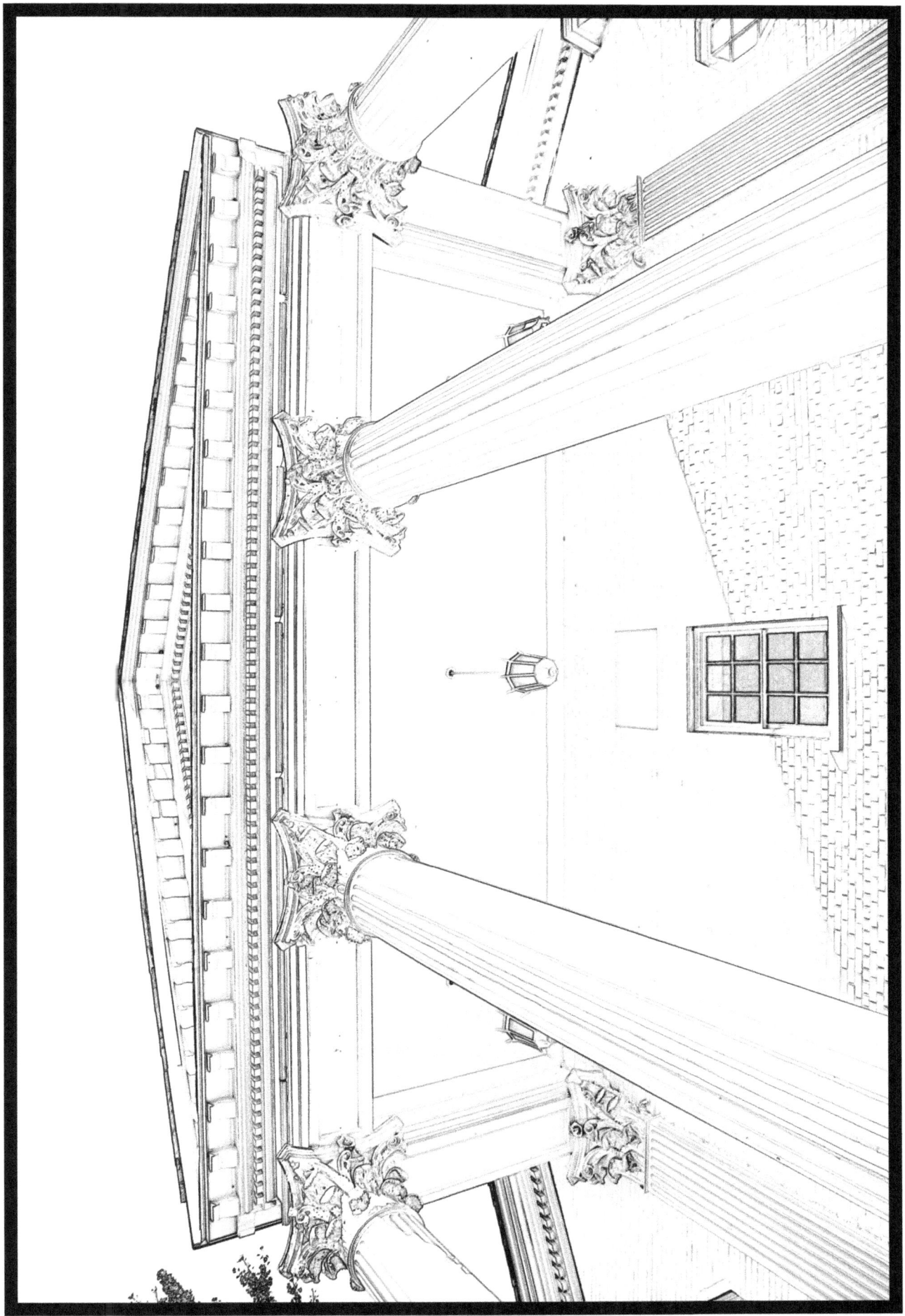

Pray out loud. Whether you're with others or alone, speak the words you're praying. It will keep you focused and will teach others — your children, other family members, friends — to pray.

Keep an open mind to how God is working in your life. He often does things in ways we are not expecting. Don't reject something just because it wasn't what you were expecting.

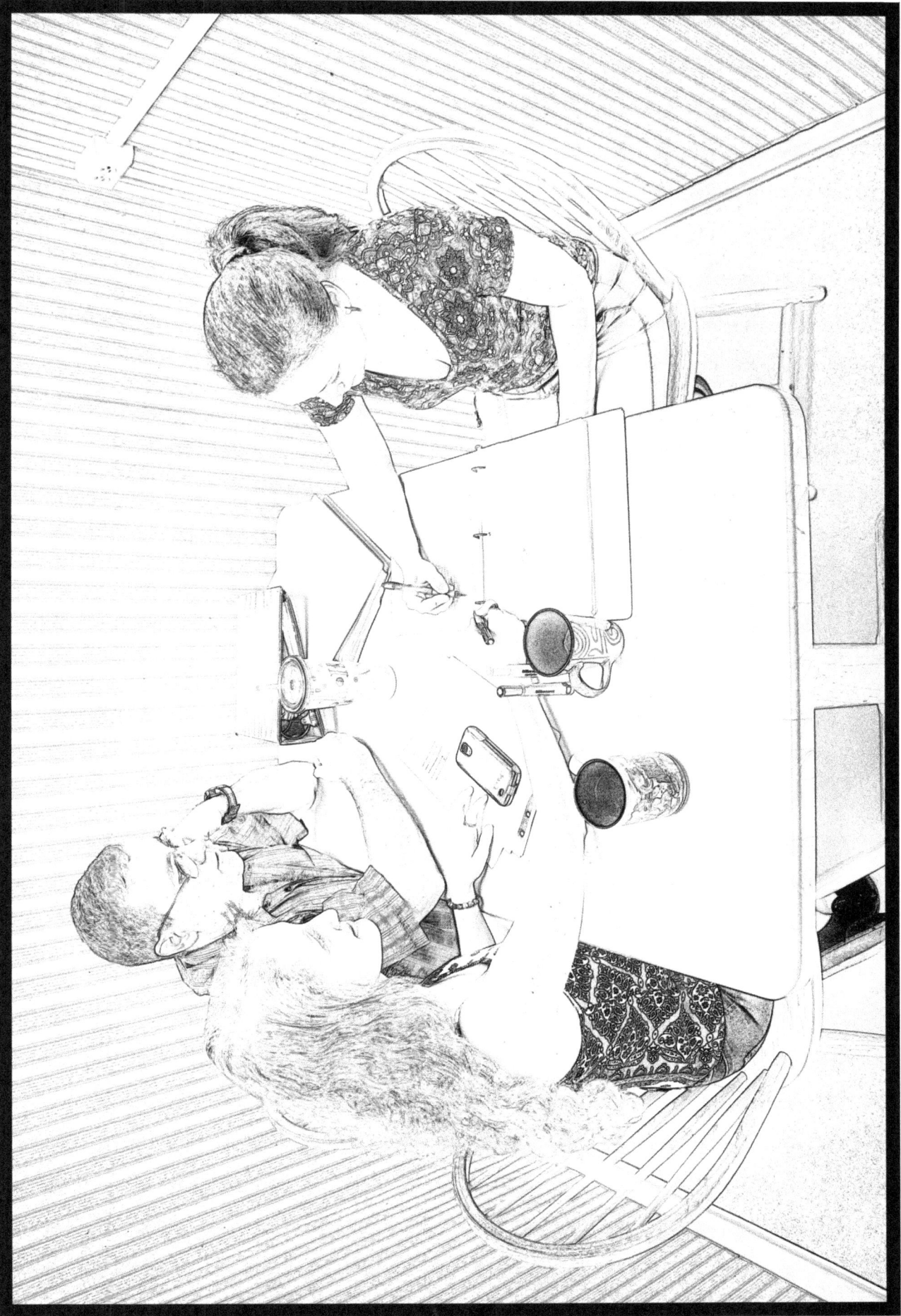

Sometimes people come into your life to help you see things from a different perspective. When they tell you their angle, even though you may disagree and it may make you angry, it's worth considering. You don't have to accept it, but it's good to understand it.

Don't choose your goals solely for the end result, choose your goals for the journey you'll have to make to reach them.

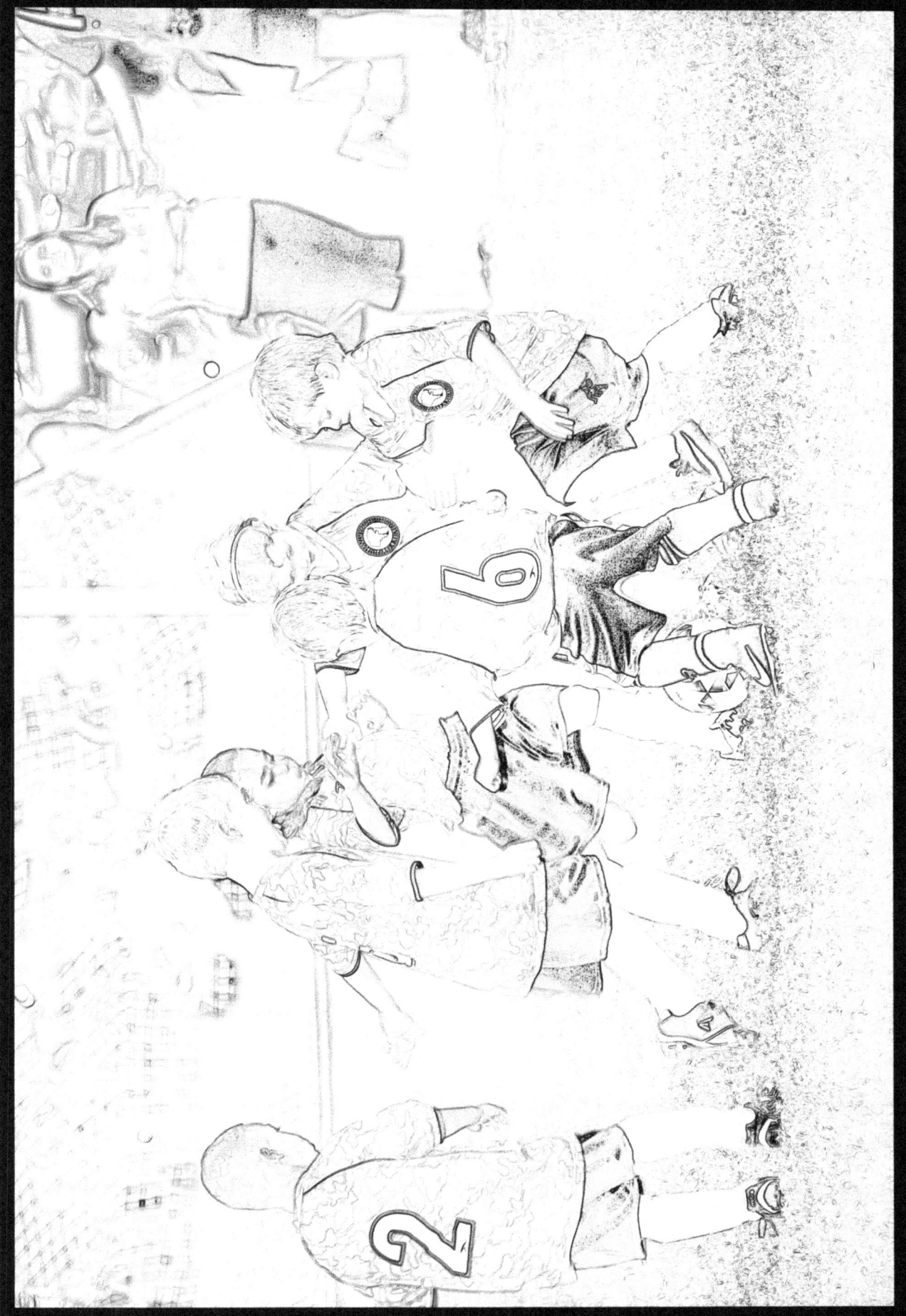

Life is like a rip current in the ocean. When you get caught in a rip current, the best thing to do is stop struggling and fighting where it's taking you. That's how you survive. You may wind up somewhere unexpected, but you'll be fine.

Always look for
the best
in whomever you
happen to be
with at the moment.
If you try, you
can find at least
one good thing,
no matter who it is
or what's happening.
It may not change
the situation, but
it will help you
deal with it.

Challenge yourself every day: How much love and kindness can you share? How will you do it?

If you can visualize it, it can happen. God will not give you a dream that won't come true if you do things His way.

You do not have to be defined by your past. Use those lessons to become the person God wants you to be today.

Beautiful things happen in our world. Bad things happen in our world. The key to dealing with everything is to never be afraid because God is always with us.

We are commanded to love one another — and that includes people who aren't good for us for a wide range of reasons. It's okay to love those people from a distance.

Don't compare yourself
to anyone else.
God made you to be
who you are:
His unique child,
with your own special
gifts and purpose.

Love people for who they are, not for who you want them to be.

No matter how much
you're hurt,
look around — the
world is still turning,
the sun still rises
and sets.
Life goes on.
Give your pain
to God.
Let Him comfort you
and use you for
His purpose.

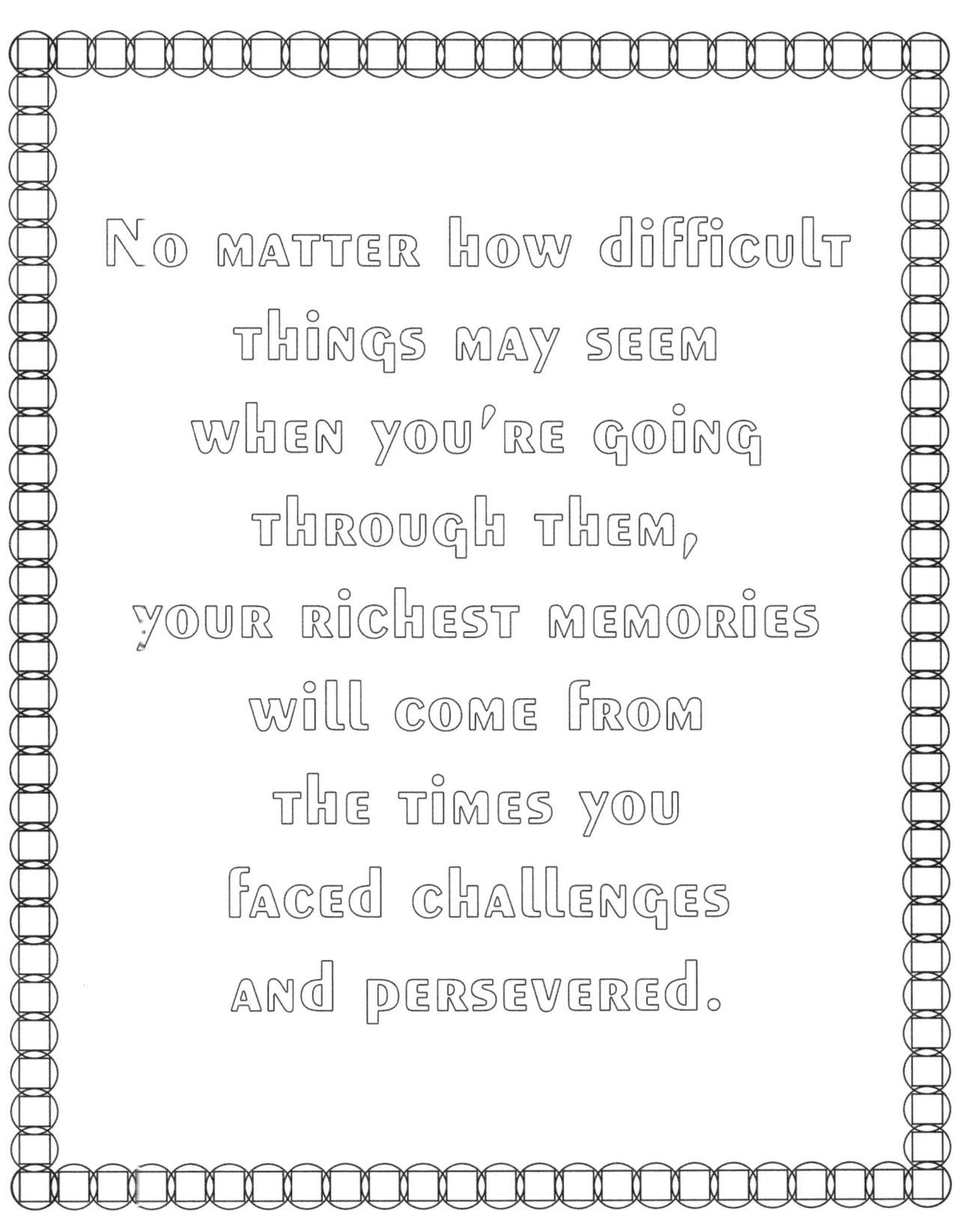

No matter how difficult things may seem when you're going through them, your richest memories will come from the times you faced challenges and persevered.

Learn to recognize true value — the value that remains when all the glitz and glitter is washed away. Don't be fooled by false worth created by artificial influences.

Love others the way you want to be loved. Love them unconditionally. Love them because of — not just in spite of — their quirks and flaws.

Be generous with praise. Express your appreciation for everything that others do for you. Let them know they have a positive impact on your life.

As you go through the day, every day, stay close to God. Listen for His voice with your head and heart. Live out His will for your life in all of your actions and thoughts.

We are the center of God's attention. He's always there, seeing everything, appreciating that His commands are being followed, grieving when they are not, and ready to step in when one of His children needs help and calls for Him.

Worldly possessions come and go.
We can lose them through no fault of our own — or by our own devices.
But wisdom, once gained, is ours to keep.
When coupled with integrity, wisdom is far more valuable than any amount of money.

We live in a world where people are often judged by their material achievements, so it's tempting to pretend we have more than we do. But living that kind of lie only leaves you empty. When we are able to be authentic and honest, our lives are far richer than when we pretend to be something we're not and have things we don't.

The past does not have to predict the future. We are new in Jesus Christ. If the past is not what you want the future to be, Jesus will help you let go of the old and create a new life in Him.

Did You Enjoy *Christian Meditations?*

Share your thoughts with others by leaving a review at
CreateTeachInspire.com/meditations

More Adult Coloring Books from Create! Teach! Inspire!

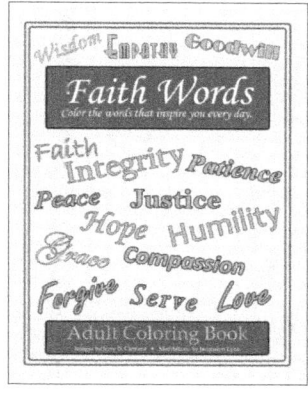
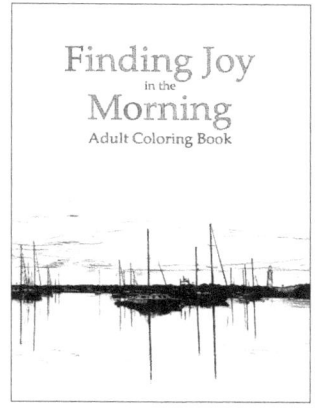
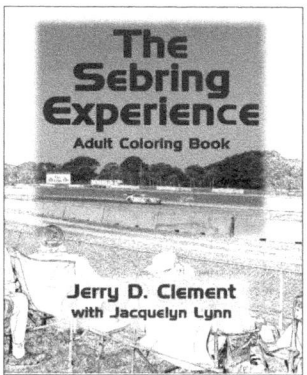

For a complete list of our available adult coloring books, visit
www.CreateTeachInspire.com/adult-coloring-books

As our thanks for your purchase, we'd like to give you five more images you can print and color. Download them now at
www.CreateTeachInspire.com/color

> For the Lord your God will bless you in all your harvest and in all the work of your hands, and your joy will be complete.
>
> *Deuteronomy 16:15b (NIV)*

Also from Create! Teach! Inspire!

Faith Works
Images for Impact
Customizable images to energize your message on social media & websites
www.CreateTeachInspire.com

Faith Works **Images for Impact** are original images you can easily customize for use on your blog, website, social media and presentations using software you probably already have on your computer.

These beautiful, high-quality photographs by Jerry D. Clement are substantially more affordable than traditional stock photography. Each collection includes five themes (sets of images), complete instructions for how to create your own custom images, and access to video tutorials.

Visit **www.FaithWorksImages.com** to see our available collections and to order.